Thrive Anyway

*12 Lessons After 12 Years of
Chronic Illness and Caregiving*

Bruce McIntyre

Rabbit Ranch Press

Edmond, Oklahoma

Thrive Anyway

Copyright © 2016 by Rabbit Ranch Press

All rights reserved. No part of this book may be reproduced or transmitted in any form or by any means without written permission from the authors.

ISBN# 978-0-9851038-2-8

Printed in the USA

Published by Rabbit Ranch Press,

A division of Creative Life Studios LLC

Cover Design by Tim Watson

Subject Headings: Family Caregiving

                       Self-Help

For more information, visit

www.BruceMcIntyre.com

Also by Bruce McIntyre

Parkinson Positive with Jerry Gill

Graceful Transition

Resilient Life

Dedication

To Kathy, Emma, and Seth. Even through adversity, you thrive anyway. You inspire me with your abundant and consistent display of grace and resilience.

Acknowledgements

The audacity of writing a book is matched only by the vulnerability of having written a book. Luckily, I have had help and encouragement along the way to refine this volume.

Rachel Cunningham contributed her impressive editorial eye to every mark of punctuation as well as the cadence, flow and tone of this book. Thank you.

Tim Watson grasped the paradoxical concept of this volume and translated it into a clean, beautiful cover.

Along our journey of chronic illness and caregiving, we have learned from some of the best including: Denise Brown, Diane Hanold, David Loftis, Jim Keating, Jerry Gill, Bob Willis, and many others.

And of course, I am grateful to our parents, Roy and Dorothy McIntyre as well as Joe and Belinda Kemp, who have helped us along our journey and modeled good caregiving.

Contents

Introduction

- 5   Denial and Resilience
- 22   Both Matter: Caregiver and Patient
- 33   Rule of 3
- 45   Say 'No' So You Can Say 'Yes'
- 52   Unexpected Blessings
- 60   Define Your Story
- 69   Find Your Partners
- 76   Keep Learning
- 83   Give and Live Beyond Yourself
- 93   Create Beautiful Moments Anyway
- 103   Determination Required
- 115   There is Grace for You
- 130   Conclusion

Introduction

Both/And. Our experience with chronic illness and caregiving has been both beautiful and devastating. Sometimes on the same day!

I suspect your experience is similar.

If you zoom out and think objectively about your situation from a big picture point of view, you tend to find the balance. However, in the daily struggles and symptoms, or during a long season of setbacks, perspective quickly fades. In this book, I am calling you to renew your perspective. Acknowledge the harsh side of reality, but intentionally take notice of and pursue those beautiful, serendipitous moments as well.

The prolonged experience of chronic illness and caregiving can be awful…miserable, terrifying, disappointing, and downright depressing. However, running parallel to this struggle I have also found unexpected joy, peace, love, and beauty. It's a paradox.

A reflection from our "pre-illness" trip to the gritty sands of Galveston Island, Texas in late 2001 captures the essence of this *both/and* notion.

Three months pregnant with our daughter and not yet showing, my wife agreed to a quick beach getaway after Labor Day. On this trip, we exercised a peaceable rhythm for mornings. After several trips together in our young marriage, we determined that we hold opposite values on how to vacation.

I awaken early…like 5:00 a.m. early… ready to go explore. My wife strongly prefers sleeping in until 9:00 a.m. and relishing in an extended rest.

This trip would be no exception.

On the second morning, I eased out for an early morning jog on the beach. With sand squishing through my toes and moist ocean air filling my lungs, I ran about a mile. Soon after the turn at the halfway mark, I paused to consider the paradox that was quickly engulfing me.

To the west, a dark, threatening storm was approaching with deep, billowing thunderclouds accented by frequent lightning. To the east, the sun began to peak up over the horizon.

Devastation and fear loomed heavily in one direction, while beauty and hope arose in the other.

Just then, something caught my eye about fifty yards out in the ocean. Two dolphins were undulating their way up the coast, jumping in and out of the water. Standing on the beach in the middle of this great enigma, I interpreted this profound moment as a clear message of *both/and*. Dark, impending storm contrasted by the hope of a beautiful sunrise. And I stood there in the middle, bewildered, with two dolphins frolicking in the waves, seemingly unfazed. What a paradox! So I just made peace with it.

Our journey of chronic illness and caregiving since 2004 has been similar and equally striking.

Moments of great beauty and gratitude seem to be countered with impending disaster and devastation. It's not *either/or*. Rather, always *both/and*.

Welcome to the struggle! I encourage you to join me in making peace with the paradox. Because as bad as some days or months can be, hope and beauty and joy can be manifested in an instant...whether by surprise or on purpose.

As my wife and I continue to learn how to live gracefully through chronic illness and caregiving, we know that you can too. Your inherent capacity for resilience will guide you as you transcend challenging circumstances.

So, join me for twelve lessons learned along the way of the past twelve years of chronic illness and caregiving. These certainly aren't the only twelve lessons we have learned, but these lessons are serving us well, and I suspect they will also be helpful to you.

You can thrive anyway!

Lesson One

Denial of the diagnosis is natural. It's just not helpful for very long.

Denial is a useful defense mechanism until it's not.

-Rosalind Kaplan

Denial does not merely tempt you upon diagnosis; it may happen with every change along the way.

When I finally came around to acknowledge the bitter realities of my wife's illness, I assumed that I had "this denial thing" licked. As it turns out, my knee jerk reaction is to avoid bad news. So, I have consistently lagged behind my wife in processing each tough change along the way.

But please relax your guilt muscle. As you will see in this chapter, denial is a natural self-defense mechanism. It's just not helpful for very long. In other words, it has a limited shelf life.

Denial As Grief Work

I love this bit of wisdom from Elizabeth Kubler-Ross, "Denial helps us to pace our feelings of grief. There is a grace in denial. It is nature's way of letting in only as much as we can handle." And grief is the appropriate word here. Any loss, including the loss of health, prompts a grief response.

On top of that, we process grief at different speeds. There exists no "one size fits all" model for grief after a death, a loss of health, or any significant life change. It just takes time to work through it. Often, the initial response of denial is one of our first steps in that direction.

This should make you feel better. Unless your spouse has been suffering from an autoimmune disease for twenty years and you still think it's all in her head. In that case, you should probably feel bad!

For the rest of us, whether we are processing the loss of normal, the loss of health, or the loss of a loved one, resisting reality for a while is natural. It's just not helpful in the long run. Of course, most of us awaken to bitter reality soon enough to move into action.

Your move from denial to action proves that you are summoning your inner capacity for resilience.

And, resilience is a much more endearing topic than denial. So, let's hunker down there for a moment.

Insights on Resilience

In her classic volume, *Strengthening Family Resilience*, Froma Walsh defines resilience as, "the ability to rebound from crisis and overcome life challenges." Some of us just want to bounce back. The truth is that after a significant life crash, our old realities do not exist anymore. Therefore, we bounce forward into new realities…or crawl, as it may be.

Since resilience may be referred to as bouncing forward when normal gets upended, there is hope. Ann Masten, in her research on resilience in children, says, "The most surprising conclusion emerging from studies of these children is the ordinariness of resilience."

Ordinary?

Did you catch that? She said the "ordinariness of resilience."

When you or I struggle with determination through years of rebuilding after a stroke, cancer, or lingering autoimmune disease, it hardly feels ordinary. Because it has taken all of the emotional, mental, spiritual, and physical energy we have.

Yet, zooming out to widen our perspective, this notion of resilience as "ordinary magic" should encourage you. This is good news. People are resilient, and so are you!

"What began as a quest to understand the extraordinary has revealed the power of the ordinary. Resilience does not come from rare and special qualities, but from the everyday magic of ordinary, normative human resources in the minds, brains, and bodies of children, in their families and relationships, and in their communities," claims Masten.

Of course, we play out the processes of resilience in our heads even as we live through it from day to day. How we think and how we talk to ourselves really matters. To dig a bit deeper into this fascinating practice, let's consider how self-talk can prompt resilience.

How Self-Talk Prompts Resilience

First of all, what is self-talk? It's that quiet voice behind our eyes that offers a running commentary on our thoughts and actions. Sometimes in the form of harsh criticism, sometimes encouragement, self-talk happens.

If you are quiet and still, you can hear it. While using affirmative thoughts to replace degrading thoughts is absolutely useful, I like the idea of interrogative self-talk.

In this more intentional style of self-talk, you ask yourself questions. You push back.

For instance, if you have worked all day, picked up the kids, gone back to the office and returned home exhausted only to find that the house is a mess, your loved one is sick in bed, and the kids have not done any homework or fed the cat, you might lose it.

Meaning, you might yell or sit down and cry.

But, what if you simply forced yourself into a few questions? Retreating to the bathroom, that sacred space of thought gathering, you might step back and ask yourself something like this:

Why is this happening? My spouse is sick and the children are children. They did not do this to me.

Why am I angry? I am tired.

Can I do this? Yes. I can't do it all at once, but I can do some.

What do I need? I need a break for 10 minutes. Then, I will get up and deal with what needs to be done, one thing at a time.

What if it all doesn't get done tonight? I will do what I can and leave the rest for tomorrow. I feel better about doing a little bit every day, than I do by procrastinating or avoiding it all together. Just make progress and love these crazy people.

This is interrogative self-talk. You question and push back and talk yourself through it. Add in some humor…and some grace. I strongly recommend that you give this a try.

Overlooking the Obvious

In care situations, which are often fraught with difficulty, we may tend to overlook the obvious. I love the way Ted Leeson, author of the classic book *The Habit of Rivers*, captures this phenomenon in two excerpts.

"Someone once asked Ray Charles what the worst part of being blind was; he replied, 'Not being able to see.' Some things are pointedly obvious, and for that reason alone are easily overlooked."

In the same vein, people often tell us the truth about themselves or their business. Under the guise of humor, sarcasm, or despair, the truth gets told. Still, we may overlook what they are obviously telling us. Typically, though, it is easy to discern if we tune in to their channel.

Leeson gives this humorous example on blatant truth telling during a trip to an Oregon greasy spoon later in his book:

"For reasons that became abundantly clear, it [the diner] announced itself with a hand lettered sign–no name, just a message: 'The Worst Food in Oregon.' This, I discovered, was no joke. The coffee might just have been the worst in the world. I ordered up the breakfast special (recorded in my notes as "Toast-and-Eggs Regret"), and under the circumstances, found it difficult to complain about the result, the cook having lived up so fully to his end of the agreement."

Did you notice how obvious Leeson's two examples are? Naturally, the worst part of being blind is not being able to see! Furthermore, if you stop at a restaurant claiming to be the worst, why would you be surprised at yucky food?

Our tendency to overlook the obvious, or to dismiss and avoid painful realities, is somewhat natural, like a self-defense mechanism. It's just not helpful for very long.

One indicator of the obvious, yet painful truths in our lives is humor. While this is a good coping mechanism, humor can also be a tip off. Over the years, I have noticed that people joke about the truth.

For instance, I had a co-worker who was unbearable. Everyone dreaded their dealing with her. One year, she dressed as a witch for Halloween. Upon entering the room, no one said a word, but looked around awkwardly. Finally, she blurted out, "Well, I'm a witch 365 days a year, but today, I thought I would dress the part."

Funny! Then again, it was true.

Another example of this phenomenon has happened to me in multiple job interviews. When the selection team jokes about difficult people or processes, they are telling the truth. Joking to blunt the pain, but telling the truth nonetheless.

Take a moment to reflect on your own present realities. Are you overlooking the obvious? If so, what do you need to do about it? Or, are you angry because of your care partner's behavior, when they are blatantly bearing their frustrations?

Worth Repeating

Sometimes the first duty of intelligent men is the restatement of the obvious.

-George Orwell

Three wakeup calls

Diagnosis Day. After several weeks of rapid muscle loss, profound soreness, and debilitating weakness, we arrived at the rheumatologist's office for the official diagnosis. For half an hour, new vocabulary whizzed past our ears, heard but not yet understood.

Essentially, we heard that the cause of Dermatomyositis is somewhat of a mystery. Moreover, the rheumatologist informed us that there was no cure yet, and that the average patient visits multiple doctors and attempts various treatments and medicinal cocktails before finding what helps control their disease. On this surreal day in 2004, we managed the doctor's consult as best we could at age thirty-one. We dutifully paid our co-pay, purchased an armful of medications, and took the long drive home rehashing and attempting to comprehend what had just happened.

"Did he say there is no cure?" I asked.

"Yes, that's what I've read also, but I have also read of some people who are in full remission," my wife assured me.

At this point in our lives, neither of us had ever had a long-term, chronic illness. So, the concept of getting sick, going to the doctor, taking medications, and NOT being soon cured was foreign to us. In fact, this notion would not fully register with us for some time.

Exhausted, but still sensing a responsibility to get back to work, I returned to my office at 3:00 p.m., gave my office assistant a recap of the day's events, and endeavored to accomplish something. At this point, I encountered my second wakeup call of the day.

Unwanted phone call. Then, the phone rang. With a distressed, yet forcibly controlled tone, my mother informed me that my best friend since kindergarten had been taken to the Vanderbilt trauma center and was tenuously holding onto life. He had been in a shooting accident, and at this point it appeared to be self-inflicted.

I hung up, gave quick explanation to my office assistant, and raced an hour and a half back to downtown Nashville, wondering if I would find my friend still alive. Knowing his family predisposition and his recent depression, I chastised myself for not preventing his desperation.

As I drove through tears, I called another friend who would meet me at the hospital. And, I hastily worked through the words to say if given the chance.

Knowing all too well the fundamentalist interpretations of both of the day's events, I practiced theological battles with any well-meaning but dogmatic souls who might be standing guard.

I affirmed what I deeply believe, "God did not strike my wife with illness due to some sin on anyone's part. No, as the old bumper sticker states so eloquently, 'shit happens', and it appears that it has happened to us. But, I will not blame God for it. Because God is with us, and will help us through this."

In preparation for the destination's end to this drive, I again affirmed, "Suicide is not the unforgiveable sin of the selfish leaving no hope for the perpetrator. No, if ever God drew near to someone in this life, surely God draws near to the person whose anguish takes them to such a desperate place as to think that this is their best option. God has not forsaken my friend, but was with him even in that terrible moment. And, I am here for him because he is my best friend and I love him."

Fortunately, my friend survived this bout with extreme depression, and we surrounded him with support and new life. And he, in turn, supported us the next several years as Kathy's disease unfolded.

Diagnosis day. It was one of the worst days of my life, compounded by the preceding scenario and this third wakeup call that followed a few weeks later.

A Punch In The Gut. Like many parents, we worked to "get our act together" before we had children. Assuming we could shield our children from unnecessary hindrances, our six and half years of marriage prior to children helped us mature our relationship, our finances, and career options. Prepared as anyone can be, we welcomed our babies into a safe home.

But, Dermatomyositis did not respect our plans. In the end, that is okay because our children have learned grace and resilience and sensitivity to people who struggle.

Still, our world was rocked by what we overheard one evening from our two and half year-old daughter mere weeks into my wife's illness.

As she had heard Kathy explain that she couldn't pick her up, Emma was learning to crawl into mom's lap and find new ways of accessing her mother's snuggles. We generally assume that children are oblivious to what the adults are talking about, but as the following scene unfolded, we learned otherwise.

Speaking to her favorite doll (Mandy was her name), our daughter calmly explained in her squeaky little voice, "Mandy, Mommy can't hold you right now because she is sick."

Listening from the back of the living room, my wife and I looked at each other with instant grief. She swept into the living room and sat beside Emma to comfort her, while I was caught off guard by a wave of emotion that sent me reeling.

Our daughter was affected whether we liked it or not. Our newborn son was affected, and in an unexpected turn of events, we learned that our daughter's baby doll was affected as well.

These three wakeup calls in quick succession hurt deeply. They also exposed a sense of my own entitlement of which I was previously unaware.

Entitlement

Perhaps it was Henri Nouwen, the prolific spiritual writer of the 20th century, who first grabbed my attention and exposed my sense of entitlement. In the context of care, I recall him pointing out that those who live with a sense of entitlement, thinking nothing bad should ever happen in their lives, are almost always bitter and resentful when bad things do happen.

Don't worry though; I haven't beaten myself up too badly about this and neither should you. I mean, seriously, isn't it a worse problem to expect that bad things WILL happen to you?

Still, entitlement issues must be managed. I found that there is another way. If we live with a sense of gratitude for what we have, however perfect or imperfect that may be, we eschew the trap of entitlement. Finding something to be grateful for every day, no matter the circumstances, is not for the shallow. Rather this intentional choice in living through caregiving or chronic illness yields defiant joy.

You have seen this in action. Going to the hospital to visit someone after heart surgery to encourage them and they convey a greater sense of peace and encouragement to you. As you leave, walking across the parking lot, you may have found yourself thinking, *wait, I came to support them, but they ministered to me!*

Or, consider this way of working through entitlement. *I did not ask for this. This was not on my bucket list. This disease and situation are not ideal; in fact, they are limiting and changing our plans. BUT, it is what we have right now. So, I am determined to do the best I can with it. I am thankful that I still have my wife and my children still have their mother. And we will love her well and receive her love well even in sickness. In fact, I am thankful for the opportunity to see life from this new perspective. It is teaching me to be more grateful and to treasure small moments. As it turns out, the best and most important moments are less about impressing other people than they are about being there, being together in the beauty that is often overlooked. So yes, I am grateful for this day. I have a contented smile that will infect those around me.*

And, I am grateful to have enough energy for the challenges of this day, because I will transcend them with peace and joy for all.

If you heard a convincing tone in that paragraph, you are correct. Often, we must intentionally talk ourselves into better ways of thinking.

Viewing the world (even in less than ideal circumstances) from a posture of gratitude and reality yields a far healthier stance than one of entitlement or doom.

Resistance

Have you ever resisted a good idea? Even if you are a fairly objective person and well-informed about your options, you may still experience a hesitation when it comes time to make a change.

What changes might you resist? Ceasing to drive, moving to a retirement community, moving in with one of your children, trying a new treatment, turning over control of your finances, signing the power of attorney, or any conflicting change such as these.

For two years Kathy's doctors suggested and strongly encouraged her to try a new IVIG infusion treatment for Dermatomyositis patients. We resisted. For two years!

Finally, we met someone at a support group who was doing this therapy. With a bit of confidence, we began. Then, after attending the national myositis convention in 2014, and meeting scores of other patients who engaged in this type of therapy, we learned of an option to receive the treatments in our own home for the same cost. These other patients referred to the IG as "liquid gold."

Now, we're not sure we want to stop! So where did the resistance come from? Early on, my wife experienced most of the side effects to one particular medication. "Most" is not an exaggeration. We checked the side effects again and checked off all of them: Hair loss, unable to sleep, vomiting, nausea, facial hair, Cushing's syndrome, etc.

This one terrible experience left us extremely hesitant about making changes when we were experiencing some stability, though that stability was slowly moving in a negative direction. Thankfully, we did muster up the courage to risk a new treatment and Kathy has had better strength and endurance because of it.

You may find yourself resisting what you know is good. If so, attempt to put your finger on the pulse of the fear that gives you pause.

Back to Denial and Resilience

Denial is a natural self-defense mechanism. It's just not helpful for very long. So, if you sense that you are slipping into chronic avoidance of the problem, summon your inner courage and call it what it is.

Identify the truth of the situation. You might even write it down or talk it out with someone. But, engage it as best you can. As M. Scott Peck reminds us, "It is only because of problems that we grow mentally and spiritually."

Unexpected low blows may knock you down, but you can get back up. You are resilient. You can do th**is**!

Lesson Two

Chronic illness is not just the patient's problem. It affects the caregiver as well.

No man is an island, entire of itself.

-John Donne

While this may seem rather obvious, it took us a while to accept. Kathy kept trying to keep her illness from affecting the rest of us, as I persisted in denial. Eventually…and not too far into eventually…we acknowledged reality.

Kathy's freedom and ability to do what she wanted had been limited, but so had mine, and so had our children's. Driving, picking up the baby, cooking dinner, working, playing in the yard…all of these mundane components of life taken for granted so easily were now out of Kathy's reach. She couldn't do these things.

I had to do them.

Thus, chronic illness is not just the patient's problem. It affects the caregiver as well.

Psychologists refer to this as one of the realities of family systems theory. In other words, no person is an island unto themselves. What affects one person also affects another.

The Protector

One of the unexpected results of caregiving arrives as you find yourself defending or protecting your loved one. For instance, *well people*, who have never experienced more than the flu, cannot adequately grasp the challenges of a chronic condition. When you simply get sick and get well within a few days or weeks, you just can't understand what it is like to not pull out of illness.

Some of the people at a church we once attended provide an example. Two of our leaders insisted on combining the teens with older adults in a mentoring setting on Sunday mornings. This is a great idea! However, when the turnout was less than what they expected, staff members surmised about people's apathy. Hearing this, I noted five to ten people who might be interested, including my wife, who could not climb the stairs.

While my explanation was given some credence initially, it was ultimately disregarded. "We can just have the teens help people up the stairs who need help," was the conclusion.

Right. This made me angry on behalf of my wife. Neither she nor some of the more elderly adults wish to struggle up the stairs every Sunday, with or without help. They do not wish to be a spectacle, and they certainly do not wish to be an object of anyone's pity.

So, in the end, they did not participate.

Most of the time, it is easy to overlook people's misunderstanding. At other times, it is simply maddening.

Such as when an employer uses guilt and shaming techniques every time you make arrangements for treatments. Not for extra days off, mind you, but just to use the days you are allotted.

If you get angry occasionally on behalf of your loved one and perhaps even take appropriate action, that's a good thing. Your protective impulse arises out of a sense of love and justice. Your caree will appreciate it. Just don't stay mad all of the time!

Affects on the Spousal Relationship

According to a study by Joan Monin on spouses expressing emotion in care scenarios, "Expressions of positive emotions have numerous interpersonal benefits, such as increasing both partners' experience of positive emotions, building relationships, and enhancing approachability."

This all makes perfect sense. We tend to respond well when we are appreciated. Granted, sternness does get our attention but it rapidly tends to grow into resentment. Thus, the proverbial honey always works better than vinegar.

I think this goes both ways. Over the years, it may become difficult to express true emotion in a relationship, chronic illness or not. But, if the caregiver can pause to offer some meaningful appreciation and support and the care recipient can pause to do the same, the relationship will have taken a step forward. This poses an important step that may propel you through the worst of times.

As the researchers suggest, "We found that care-recipients who were more willing to express happiness had spouses who reported less insensitive responding."

The challenge here is the difficulty of expressing happiness when you feel miserable. Still, to the extent the patient can express some happiness, the care scenario becomes more manageable and that feeling yields less burnout, insensitivity, and resentment.

The researchers go on to note, "When vulnerable emotions, such as sadness, fear, and anxiety, are expressed, caregivers are likely to interpret these expressions as indicators of need and to respond with support."

We seem to be wired to want to help. But, if negative emotions are the only expression that a caregiver encounters, they will soon grow weary.

All in all, these conclusions are rather obvious. So, why include them here? Simply put, we all need a reminder to treat others as we would like to be treated. Even through the pain, frustration, and discomfort of chronic illness and caregiving, kind words help.

Changing Identity

An interesting piece in the *Journal of the American Society on Aging* describes caregiving as, "a process of changing identity." Here, the authors point out that, "the caregiving role emerges from an existing role relationship. The caregiving role should not be seen as a new role that is added, but rather is most usefully viewed as the transformation of an existing role."

Specifically, the caregiver is affected as the ailing spouse moves through phases of heightened need for care. From doctor's appointments, to more intense care, to personal grooming, to a point that perhaps the caregiving role now accounts for 50% or more of the relationship.

I spoke with some caregivers about this progression and heard tales that put a fine point on the sense of losing their partner. When your lifelong co-decision maker and companion becomes more like a child, the relationship experiences a difficult transition.

It is grief.

But, the patient's role is also changing. In cases where the changes are more physical than mental, the sense of change is even more acute for the patient. They are aware that you have to work, do the cleaning, groom them, change geriatric diapers, etc.

And this is grief for the patient.

If you have shared life for decades together, as equally capable partners, the onset of limits, physically or mentally, introduces an unwelcome change to the relationship. And frankly, this becomes a source of stress unto itself.

Latent, Persistent Stress

To put a finer point on it, after a certain amount of time, I realized that I had a profound sense of latent, persistent stress. It is not good for me, just as it is not good for you. Perhaps you identify with some of the following stressors.

The stress of the constant stream of medical bills takes its toll, not only on your finances, but on your sense of hope to ever be free of these undesirable costs.

Maybe you sense that you are always doing less than you had imagined you would do together. Limitations mar our vision of the life we anticipated.

Perhaps you are tired of making excuses to avoid events for which you simply do not have the energy anymore. Or, you're weary of watching your loved one's gradual decline. Really, it's exhausting.

As a patient, you may be fatigued by your own list of things you'd like to do, but just can't. Maybe you're tired of seeing your loved one sacrifice or make accommodations for you rather than proceeding as "normal families" do. Knowing you might have done more had it not been for this illness, you may wrestle with anger and sadness.

The treatments, weakness, and ever-present disease…these are tiresome. The medications, trips to the pharmacy, hours spent in doctors' waiting rooms, training new nurses every year…again, the drain of these experiences for patient and caregiver, even for the most optimistic souls, is difficult to underestimate.

STATS

According to an article by Mickey Hinds in LIFE Senior Services Vintage Magazine in the June 2015 edition:

- 53% of caregivers report that their own health has deteriorated since becoming a caregiver
- 72% of family caregivers report not going to the doctor as often as they should
- 55% say they skip their own doctor appointments entirely
- 63% of caregivers report having worse eating habits compared to non-caregivers
- 58% indicate they have worse exercise habits than before they assumed caregiving responsibilities
- 1 in 3 caregivers report symptoms of depression
- 30% of spousal caregivers are more likely to die before the person for whom they are caring.

Clearly, chronic illness is not just the patient's problem. Family members are affected, sometimes as adversely as the patient.

Tolerated Ones and Loved Ones

But, what about problem patients? Or, problem caregivers for that matter? While we typically refer to the patient as our "loved one," some caregivers have "tolerated ones" and some patients have inattentive caregivers. It's true. Not ideal, but true in some cases.

So, what do you do? You probably have some things that bug you. For instance, my patient…

- Won't take her medicine on time
- Doesn't exercise
- Refuses to eat healthy foods
- Isn't forthright with the doctor

Or, my caregiver…

- Doesn't anticipate my needs
- Still doesn't do his share of the chores
- Has never really learned very much about my condition or medicines

And so, we affect each other's lives. For better and for worse, we really do.

The truth is that some of you have tolerated ones, rather than loved ones, at least some of the time. In these cases, a serious illness does not make your relationship better. Typically, it only exacerbates the problems that already exist.

But, you feel stuck. Maybe you are to an extent. Within every situation, some choices still remain, even if few.

Is there another family member who can help?

Could you inquire about a counselor, minister, or aging professional to whom you can talk and receive guidance?

Is it time to hire help or access services to which you are entitled?

Granted, easy answers may be scarce. But, keep inquiring to find the best possible solution.

Brave Enough to Care

Short term adversity calls on our sense of courage, but so does long term adversity; perhaps more so.

When faced with years and even decades of a chronic condition, both patient and caregiver experience the gamut of mental, emotional, spiritual, and physical challenges. Naturally, there is an ebb and flow over time. When one partner struggles, the other must be able to carry on. And vice versa.

Today may be one of those days. Now may be one of those times. So, remember, you are brave about many things.

Brave enough to care.

Brave enough to try the new therapy, new treatment…to try one more time.

Brave enough to ask the question that makes you vulnerable, to ask for help.

Brave enough to be there, to listen, to accompany, to look eye to eye.

Brave enough to learn, to connect, to refuse to give up.

You are brave. As you lean in and live into your next step that seems frightening, may you remember that you can do it, because deep down within, you are brave.

Worth Repeating

In the flush of love's light, we dare be brave. And suddenly we see that love costs all we are, and ever be. Yet it is only love which sets us free.

-Maya Angelou

Lesson Three

Follow the Rule of 3

Self-care is not selfish. You cannot serve from an empty vessel.

-Eleanor Brown

Rule 1: Do something for yourself, by yourself at least weekly if not daily.

When my wife, Kathy, gets home, we all know that this is her time. Since we have a garden tub, she can pour a nice hot bath and slip in up to her chin. Neither child nor husband dares to enter or interrupt her relaxation time!

I doubt if she has even missed ten of these divine, daily soaks in the past twelve years. This is her daily therapy. Along with reading books at night, doing yoga (for non-stretchy people) three mornings per week, and taking occasional walks, Kathy does something for herself by herself every day. And she is all the better for it!

Most mornings, I wake up by 6:00 a.m. If I am tired or resist, I remind myself to "get up and get out." Deep down, I know that if I can muster the energy to get up and get out, I will be glad I did.

Some mornings, this includes a jog or bike ride. But almost all mornings, I at least get up and walk around our neighborhood greenbelt.

A few days each week, I also do strength exercise and stretching/yoga. On special occasions, I go camping with the kids or take a longer hike.

Finding Your Transports to Joy

I love this suggestion and language from Gail Sheehy: "Reconnect with your transports to joy." Beautiful. But, how do you do it and what does this mean?

What transports you to joy? What fills your cup? Long walks, music, art, reading, cooking, or creating help many people. In order for you to reconnect with your transports to joy, you must ruthlessly carve out a sacred space and time to engage in these life-giving moments.

Yes, I realize that time may be hard to find. But, if you are going to live well through this situation or season of challenge, you must allow yourself space. Remember, you have permission to care for yourself.

So, go find your transports to joy!

Worth Repeating

Your sacred space is where you can find yourself again and again.

–Joseph Campbell

Relaxing By Being Present

Cool morning waves washed up to my ankles, occasionally surprising my knees with an unexpected surge. Wet sand slid between my toes, as the morning breeze cured something deep within me.

As sunlight slowly illuminated the shore, sandpipers and other birds scouted for their breakfast. Walkers and joggers increased as the early morning wore on, in search of peace, wholeness, and beauty. Quietly and kindly acknowledging each other in passing, we have an understanding about this sacred and fleeting time of day.

"It is good to be here, right now," I thought to myself. "The future is in the future and the past is in the past. And I am right here now."

The present brings a sense of relaxation and rest and contentment.

The magic of these moments arrives with consistency. Sure, finding your transport to joy or doing something for yourself by yourself one time is helpful.

But when you incorporate these rhythms into your life on a regular daily or weekly basis, you begin to reap the results over time like compound interest on an investment.

Therefore, you have permission to take care of yourself.

Worth Repeating

Sometimes the most important thing in a whole day is the rest we take between two deep breaths.

-Etty Hillesum

Rule 2: Connect with people who fill your cup.

We all have people who fill our cups and people who drain our cups. Some are life-giving; some are depressing. Think about the people in your life. Who fills your cup?

Breakfast friends, dinner friends, card playing friends, or book club friends…support groups, spiritual groups, exercise therapy groups, or classes…this is where you find your people. Perhaps you have a phone friend that you can't talk to about your situation at all, and this is exactly the reason you need to talk with them! Or maybe you email with someone who shares your plight and you consider her one of your best friends even though you've never met.

The point is clear. Proactively move towards the people who fill your cup. Initiate contact. Ask for time together. But, don't just take. Give them a listening ear and an encouraging word in the process. Mutual friendships tend to last much longer than one-way relationships.

Solitude differs wildly from loneliness. You may seek solitude proactively, sometimes by retreating to the woods or by creating a sacred space for renewal, prayer, and meditation. Solitude can heal the soul and bring clarity to your thoughts preparing you to re-engage with people again.

Loneliness, on the other hand, happens with much less joy. As we withdraw, we find we exclude ourselves. If we isolate ourselves long enough and resist interaction, we enter into loneliness. It comes about less proactively, and manifests as more of a gradual downward spiral.

Loneliness does not exclusively speak to being around people or not. You can be lonely in a crowd if you persistently resist connection.

As a patient or a caregiver, the impulse to pull away will likely occur at some point. But, know the difference. Engage solitude, resist loneliness, and pursue good connections.

The Connection I Didn't Know I Needed

I have always known that a good support group can help most people. I never assumed that I would need one, however. (Yes, I tend to be a slow learner.)

When my wife learned about a Dermatomyositis support group in Wichita, Kansas, I supported her decision to make the two-and-a-half-hour trip. Determining not to say anything, I prepared myself to listen, learn, and stand behind my wife.

As expected, patients explained their experience and the treatments they were engaging with various levels of success. What I did not expect was that the caregivers took their turns to speak as well.

When my turn came around, I only made a few statements. Primarily, this was due to the lump in my throat. But, the sense of burden that these few sentences relieved in me was profoundly therapeutic.

It is difficult to explain how powerful a healthy support group can be. Identifying with people who speak your language, understand your plight, and extend compassion is extremely valuable. Listening and returning encouragement and grace yields an equal amount of significance.

These trips to Wichita have been nice getaways for my wife and I, but they have also provided education, support, and hours of conversation.

About three years into my wife's Dermatomyositis, we were a part of a small group who asked us to share our story. Since they were receiving piecemeal components of our journey each week, they wanted to hear the whole story.

So, we composed a 20-minute presentation of "7 Pivotal Days on Our Journey." From diagnosis through denial on to disappointments and triumphs, we brought them up to that current moment. Granted, they laughed some at appropriate points, and wiped away tears as well. But as planned, we left them hopeful.

That night opened up a new level of sharing and trust in our group and we have forever been grateful to sojourn with them during that season of life.

Wired to Love

She had been stung.

By life, not a bee. In fact, a bee sting might have been easier.

Through a series of unfortunate events, she realized one morning that she was isolated and lonely. In retrospect, it was understandable.

She had cared for her husband, who had Alzheimer's, for almost two decades. Along the way, she had retired from her work, and due to a cross-country move, her old support network became more distant.

Now in a season of aftercare, working through her grief, she admitted to herself that she was lonely. But in that confessional instant, she sensed another strong impression.

She was wired to love.

And so, on that day, she re-engaged. She decided to make the first call, the first move with old friends, children, grandchildren, cousins, and a group of acquaintances with the promise of new friendship.

She admitted to me one spring afternoon, "I decided that if I want friends, I need to be a friend. So, I am making the first move. I am wired to love and connect, even though I am an introvert."

Pretty wise lady…with good advice for us all.

Worth Repeating

My best friend is the one who in wishing me well wishes it for my sake.

-Aristotle

Rule 3. Smart people ask for help.

A few months into Kathy's illness, someone insisted that our church would bring meals over. As simple as this may sound, I had great difficulty with this notion.

Why? Because I am a helper, not a helpee. Well, at least that's what I thought back then. As it turns out, everyone can use some help sometimes. Perhaps in the form of a consult, food, advice, education, respite, etc. But, smart people ask for help.

After a few weeks of meals being brought to our house, I announced that we did not need meals any more. We were fine. Of course, we were not.

The following Tuesday night, our friend Ann showed up at our house with five frozen meals.

"Ann, thank you so much, but you must not have heard the announcement. We're fine now, but thank you so much for bringing these meals," I explained, quite certain that this would satisfy her.

She looked me sternly in the eyes and jokingly pointed at my chest, "I know your wife is still sick, and I know you can't cook. So, I'm bringing meals until I think she is well!"

"Yes, ma'am," I answered weakly, but gratefully.

And Ann brought us meals for many weeks to come as we continued to struggle through the early months of chronic illness.

I would wish for everyone to have an Ann in her life who insists on helping you through adversity.

About a year earlier, I had sat with Ann on a few occasions as her husband struggled with prostate cancer and finally passed away. She was returning the favor and our words fall far short of describing our appreciation for her.

Even Counseling

I have always thought that counseling was a good idea for other people. As it turns out, it helped me as well! One day early on, in the worst three years of Kathy's illness thus far, a lady came to see me. As she described the situation with her mother literally at death's door and her daughter newly diagnosed with a rare autoimmune disease, I easily recognized that she was depressed.

So, we set her up to see someone and helped her subsidize the payments. She was moved to tears with gratitude, and as she left my office I leaned back against my door, exhausted by a sudden burst of reality.

"She's not the only one," I thought to myself. "I am depressed too."

Typically, I have a rather buoyant, upbeat demeanor. But, after this prolonged period of living in survival mode and keeping a tight cap on the bottle of my thoughts and emotions, I was depressed. Eventually, I acted on this realization and utilized my Employee Assistance Program (EAP) benefit to seek counseling. I needed to talk to someone.

And talk I did. I recall that first meeting quite vividly. Pouring out my story, admitting all of my stressors, and explaining my thoughts, the seasoned therapist across from me welcomed me with a nonjudgmental presence. What a relief! Simply getting it all off of my chest relieved a weighty burden and added new perspective.

With simple suggestions, he guided me back to a sense of normalcy and confidence. No longer constantly overwhelmed, I was able to move forward in my life with greater clarity. It's not that he said much that I didn't already know, it's just that I needed to say it all and receive some guidance.

I have forever been grateful for this seasoned therapist and for my own willingness to ask for help.

Desmond Tutu writes about a term for this: unbuntu. Essentially, he describes this notion as, "A person is a person through other persons. We need other humans for us to learn how to be human."

As it turns out, the *what* that we need is often a *who*.

Back to the Rule of 3

What are you doing for yourself by yourself every day or every week?

Are you connecting with individuals or groups who fill your cup?

What is the help that you need to ask for right now?

Lesson Four

Learn to say "no" so you can say "yes".

Learn to say "no" to the good, so you can say "yes" to the best.

--John Maxwell

Some days the patient has more energy than others. On our 10th anniversary, my wife shared the spoon theory with me. This story originates with Christine Miserandino at ButYouDontLookSick.com.

Here's the theory in condensed form.

Spoon Theory

A lady who was living with a debilitating autoimmune disease went to have lunch with a longtime friend. Though the friend was aware of her illness and even quite compassionate, she asked, "What's it like? I mean, I know you have this disease, but can you explain what it's like?"

If you are living with an autoimmune disease, you know just how maddening it can be to try to explain muscle soreness, weakness, and energy swings from day to day. Unlike more concrete conditions, the ebb and flow of energy can be vexing.

So, the lady with the condition explained, "Suppose you have 12 spoons to represent your energy each day. Getting ready, making breakfast, getting the kids off to school…three spoons gone. Work, meetings, and more typically consume the rest of the spoons. Some days, I don't start with 12 spoons. Some days, it's 7 or even 5."

As she explained, she was careful not to sound like a victim. Rather, she just wanted to describe what life was actually like with her condition.

As she finished her allegory of the spoons, her friend was in tears. She made the connections and began to grasp the chasm of difference between her levels of *well person* energy with that of her friend with the autoimmune disease.

She finally understood, at least in part, what it is like to live with an autoimmune disease. Whether you are living with cancer, a heart related condition, neurological disease, or any other health challenge, you can probably identify with the difficulty of explaining what it's like for you on a daily basis. Lean in. Simplify. Help people understand.

Prioritizing

We have always been "yes" people. Will you go out to eat with us? Yes. Would you like to help with our event? Yes. Can you serve on our team? Yes. We're all going to the thing this weekend, do you want to come? Yes.

With Kathy's illness, we had to learn to say "no." We didn't want to say "no," we had to say "no." Here's what we learned that may help you:

1. Clarify your priorities. Talk about what is most important to you with the people who are most important to you. Write them down. Put them in order. Your list may develop something like this: Family, Work, etc.
2. Practice saying "no." If you are not a "no" person, this will require some work. Some of you are already good at deflecting invitations you don't want, some of us are not. So, practice saying "no." This may sound silly, but have your partner or friend ask questions like the ones above. Can you help with the event? Oh, thank you so much for asking, but I can't this time.
3. Pour yourself into your priorities. Really. Try it. Whether you utter a polite no, or a triumphant and emphatic NOOOO!, you'll find it quite liberating.

Once you've done this, you actually pour yourself into your priorities. See, this isn't just saying "no" for the sake of itself. Rather, you are making a proclamation of freedom. Even with unwelcome health conditions, limited finances, or increased responsibilities and stress...especially with these, you need to run to your highest priorities.

If you're still having trouble deciding what your priorities are, perhaps the following thoughts will help you gain clarity.

Words from the End

What do people talk about at the end?

In *The Mayo Clinic Guide to Stress-Free Living,* Kerry Egan, a hospice chaplain describes what she has learned:

"They talk about the love they felt, and the love they gave. Often they talk about love they did not receive, or the love they did not know how to offer, the love they withheld, or maybe never felt for the ones they should have loved unconditionally."

In all of the hectic grasping for what we want out of life, sometimes we miss the point of life. Prioritizing becomes much clearer from the perspective of your last sunrise and sunset.

So, this is a good reminder for me, and I hope that it is for you.

Worth Repeating

The best thing to hold onto in life is each other.

−Audrey Hepburn

Isn't it amazing how easily less important things squeeze into our lives and crowd out the things and people and thoughts that we really want to invest our lives into? Having looked at this from a view from the end, let's try another angle from the garden.

Weed and Feed

One Saturday, I did a four-hour meditation on weeds.

This mental/spiritual exercise was aided by the fact that I was literally pulling weeds in our yard for those four hours! We loved the May showers, but since I didn't do much tidying up during May, the weeds had grown strong.

And this is how it is. The weeds of debt, toxic relationships, resentment, laziness, etc. tend to grow unless we do regular maintenance to eliminate them.

Of course, I have noticed in my front yard that with ample water and fertilizing, the grass grows deep green and strong, with minimal need for weed pulling. So, feeding is crucial as well.

I suggest that you feed…

- Your heart with people who contribute life to your life
- Your soul with spiritual space
- Your mind by learning and engaging your curiosity
- Your body with fresh foods, rest, and regular exercise
- Weed and feed. It's not just for your lawn.

Remaining in the garden for a while, these next thoughts on pruning first appeared in my blog. But, I think as you consider the dynamics of pruning, you will be drawn into a quick correlation for your own life, lending you perspective on saying "yes" and "no."

Pruning

The moist smell of cool, morning, summer air stirred lightly past my nostrils and I breathed it in… deeply.

Pepper, our cat, was playing with an unlucky toad. A young robin kept an eye on the cat as it pecked at the bird feeder. The steady sound of water trickling down our fountain provided the perfect backdrop for nature's symphony as birds chatted, bickered, and issued feline warnings.

Orange carnations and red climbing roses were peeking out again after rainfall from the previous night that offered a break to the relentless heat. Even the pigeon cooing from the power line had a calming effect on my soul as it harmonized with our bamboo wind chimes.

6:15 a.m.

I was so thankful to be in that moment. And I was so thankful that the pruning worked.

As I had pruned back the rose bushes some time earlier, I worried that they might never grow back again. But, since I didn't really prune them much at all the previous season and the blooms were dismal, I had no choice. I had to try.

It seemed counterintuitive to cut them back…to prune. But on that morning in that sacred space, I witnessed the beautiful bounty of rose bushes made possible in part by pruning.

And so it is with our own lives. On a regular basis, we need to reflect and choose what needs pruning. Sometimes a strong "no" yields a bountiful "yes."

Lesson Five

Be open to unexpected blessings

A wonderful gift may not be wrapped as you expect.

-Jonathan Lockwood Huie

When we moved back to Oklahoma City to live with Kathy's parents for a while, I knew it was the right thing to do at the time. I had no doubt. My wife would have the time and space to recover, and my children would have four adults in the house to love on them at the ages of four and one.

I knew this. And, as I watched our children snuggle with their Granny and wrestle in the floor with their Pa, I realized that their cups were being filled far better than I had been able to do by myself. For this, I am thankful.

Long Drives

That being said, living with your in-laws is not for the faint of heart! So, I had my escape plans always ready. As I activated these plans, I typically regained a larger perspective. When I got up for early morning jogs or loaded up the kids for evening drives around a nearby lake, I discovered beauty along the way. And in turn, I glimpsed the big picture for which I was grateful.

Long drives, walks, and jogs are good medicine for the soul. This rhythm was crucial for this short season of life.

And in a larger sense, many of the blessings we experienced were somewhat unexpected. The kindness of so many friends, as well as the new sources of encouragement we met along the way both came as a bit of a surprise. In retrospect, we may have been inadvertently positioning ourselves for these waves of refreshment.

In your care situation, you may find that some of the following perspectives help you posture yourself to be receptive to unexpected blessings.

Giving Thanks by Mental Subtraction

Have you ever arrived at gratitude via the side door or perhaps the back door? Here's what I mean.

As Christopher Peterson articulates, "It may matter whether we think about the good things in our lives in terms of their presence (e.g., I have a great job) or in terms of their absence (e.g., Suppose I did not have this great job). Research participants who did mental subtraction rated the good event in question as more surprising than those who simply thought about the good event. This wonderful thing- my job, my spouse, my good health-did not have to happen."

In other words, think of one thing that you are most grateful for: the chance to take a certain vacation, recovery from an illness, an unexpected gift, a treasured relationship, etc. Perhaps you are grateful to be finding life again in the midst of illness. One thing.

Now, what if this had not happened? Go ahead, try it. I'll wait.

No seriously, try it.

Doesn't this exercise awaken your gratitude molecules? You might even physically experience a tingly feeling of enlivened appreciation.

Giving thanks by subtraction. Add this to your toolbox!

Worth Repeating

We often take for granted the very things that deserve our gratitude.

-Cynthia Ozick

3 Secrets to Perseverance

Empty tank, overdrawn account, too much on your plate; it happens to pretty much everyone at some point along the way.

And there are certainly more than 3 secrets to perseverance through adversity. But, here are 3 to get you started:

1. *Hit the "REFRESH" button.* Get up, get out, and renew your perspective. Exercise, pray, journal, or howl at the moon! Trade out the self-defeating self-talk for intentionally hopeful and truthful messaging. Yes, this requires a bit of persistence and determination on your part. Some folks have lists of messages they refer to in their Evernote app, journal, or sticky notes. Others use affirming passages of scripture and spiritual messages. If you are slugging your way through a particularly tough season, you may need to hit the RERESH button several times per day, but don't give up!

2. *Remember past perseverance.* You've made it through challenging times before. So, you can do it again. Remember that experience and what helped you survive last time.

3. *Decide what you're going to do and do it.* Whoa! Don't make a list of thirty-one things. Make a list of one to three things that you can do today and do them. As you act on what you have decided, you will feel better and make progress in the right direction.

You have enough energy, faith, and courage for today!

Worth Repeating

Perseverance is not a long race; it is many short races one after the other.

-Walter Elliot

Survivor Tree Reflections

On April 19, 1995, I was on the phone with a college bookstore in California when our office building shook and some of the windows blew out. I was working in downtown Oklahoma City.

During those first days and weeks, we learned of staggering loss. Everyone was affected. In fact, I have yet to find anyone living in Oklahoma City at that time that wasn't in some way connected. Though the loss of life was tremendous and grief remains, our fine city has never been the same. We are better.

A few years ago, I finally dared to step onto the Oklahoma City National Memorial. There, I became reacquainted with that American elm...placed in pictures as far back as 100 years ago. It took the brunt of the blast. Some wanted to push it over, but others insisted on nurturing it back to health.

They removed the debris and created space for healing in order to coax life back into it. Slowly, the tree began to thrive again. On the very day that you are reading this, several hundred people will have walked past and considered this tree...the Survivor Tree. Having seen no city, the rise of a city, as well as good, bad, and ugly, the Survivor Tree still stands and inspires others. This tree is resilient!

And so are you.

At least once a year, I sit with the Survivor Tree to meditate. I have taken support groups there. And if you happen to be in Oklahoma City, I recommend that you take a few moments of your life to spend some time with this tree.

Just as the Survivor Tree is resilient and has been nurtured back to life with the help of others, so can YOU! If this tree can even inspire others with its story, so can YOU!

Worth Repeating

Surviving is important; thriving is elegant.

-Maya Angelou

A Litany of Unexpected Blessings

Kathy and I awoke on the first day of the 2014 Myositis National Conference in Reno, Nevada to find hundreds of hot air balloons out our hotel window. On a whim three days later, we rented an extremely small rental car to drive an hour into the Sierra Nevada Mountain range to see Lake Tahoe.

While we gained an immense amount of helpful information at the conference, the hot air balloons and the drive around Lake Tahoe were two unexpectedly wondrous bonuses of the trip.

Several years ago, I was on my way to speak at a caregiving seminar at a local university. Unfortunately, I was in a bad mood. Therefore, I swung through Starbucks looking for a "pick me up."

Much to my surprise, I experienced an immediate day changer. As I approached the drive-thru window, the barista informed me that the lady in front of me did random acts of kindness in her father's memory each year on his birthday, even though he had passed on. She had paid for my coffee! This instant joy was matched as I offered to pay for the person behind me.

This has happened to me five times as of this writing and once for frozen yogurt.

Similar experiences are awaiting you!

Whether you run into old friends in unexpected locations or take brief ice cream runs with your beloved that turn into meaningful conversations, blessings await.

When they happen, simply receive and be grateful.

Lesson Six

Define your story

Sometimes reality is too complex. Stories give it form.

-Jean Luc Godard

People never seem to ask when you're ready for them. These surprise attacks can happen in waiting rooms, on elevators, or in the bleachers. "What's wrong with your hands? Does your mother have Alzheimer's? Why were you in the hospital?"

In response, we often stammer and say things we don't really want to say. But, we say them enough that we begin to believe them.

So, I suggest that you write out one paragraph to explain your situation on your terms. Tell it the way you want it to be told, or at least tell it the way you hope for it to be.

For instance, *I have Parkinson's disease. That's why I move slower and have this tremor. But, I am learning more and I do exercise and voice therapy. These have taught me that I have more control over this disease than I thought. I may have Parkinson's, but Parkinson's doesn't have me!*

Or, *my wife has Dermatomyositis. It affects her muscles and skin and she has had it for twelve years. At first it was terrible, but she is better now and she even teaches first grade. So, while it's been up and down and she is still only about 70% of where she was before this illness, we're thankful for what we've learned along the way, for the people we've met, and hopeful that we've been able to help others along their way.*

I love the way comedian Amy Poehler puts it, "You are more than this one story of crisis."

You have had good and bad happen. You have caused wonderful things to happen in the world, and you may have also caused some hurt feelings. You have won and been triumphant. You have reached some of your goals. You have done a lot of good stuff!

And this one thing also happened. True, it has greatly affected your life in ways you had not foreseen. But, your story is about more than this one crisis, more than this condition, more than this moment in time.

So, think of your story in context. Not just what great things you did before, but what great things you are doing with and through and beyond these difficult circumstances.

Rebounding From Adversity

What adversity have you faced in your life?

Think for a moment, perhaps back even forty years, of all types of challenges you have faced in your life.

It may be that some experiences got the best of you, but I would be very surprised if you hadn't ultimately or eventually overcome some significant adversity at some point along the way.

What did it take to get through it? Faith, grace, determination, assistance, hard work, forgiveness, resilience? I suspect it took a mix of many of these.

Now, what adversity are you currently facing? How will you dig deep and draw on those same resources to overcome once again?

Froma Walsh says that resilience can be defined as, "the capacity to rebound from adversity strengthened and more resourceful."

Embrace this idea! You can do it! If you get knocked down, you get back up again and in so doing, you live out your capacity for resilience.

Worth Repeating

If you will call your troubles experiences, and remember that every experience develops some latent source within you, you will grow vigorous and happy, however adverse your circumstances may seem to be.

-John Heywood

Seven Pivotal Days

Think back over the course of your illness or caregiving experience. What have been the seven most crucial days?

Most people gravitate to days like these:

- Diagnosis day
- Facing reality day
- Second crash day
- Profound accepting of help day
- Substantial milestone day
- Funerals, moves, or big events

As you craft your story, you might consider these aspects:

Physical. Since you are reading this book, physical ailment has almost certainly been part of the equation for you or your caree. So, think about it. What has changed? Functionally, what have the effects been? But also, how are you making progress and how are you attacking the problem? Please understand that most folks can only take a small amount of explanation about physical hurts and pains. So, while this may be the primary experience that you are having, be careful to limit how much you talk about it. You don't want to hold people hostage against their will! So, what is a sentence or two about your condition to help people understand, and what are you doing about it?

Social. How has this condition affected your social life? For yourself, acknowledge which friends have stepped up and which ones have disappeared. Who are you getting together with these days? Who encourages you? In what ways are you still able to encourage others? When you think of prioritizing important activities in your life, what are the most important ways to spend your energy?

Emotional. Are you crying more? Laughing again? Have you ever noticed that when you haven't laughed much in a long time, your face hurts when you finally do? Unused or under exercised laughing muscles cause this phenomenon. Who or what makes you smile that contented smile that betrays an underlying peace and joy? Whose behavior causes that maddening flare up to happen within you? How are you doing emotionally?

Mental. What ruts do you have? Are they getting deeper? What ignites your mind and causes you to engage, consider and learn? What are you thinking about most of the time? Can you identify your stressors and possible next steps to move in the right direction for each stressor?

Vocational. Are you still working? Did you have to quit your job? Does work provide an escape? Are you taking too many days off? Is your work having a positive or negative effect on your care situation?

Someone will ask. Most likely, it will not happen at a convenient time or place. They will not give you forewarning.

What will you say?

Will you have a one sentence or one paragraph answer for the airport, the restaurant, or the waiting room? Will you have an intentionally honest yet hopeful story for the few people who want to hear your 20-minute version?

By preparing and thinking through your story, you not only deliver more helpful words to other people, you are taking charge of your own story.

You are shaping the way you think about it. You are casting the story that you are living into. And you are learning to be the hero rather than the victim of the story you tell.

Challenge, Choice, Outcome

As you grapple with the disorientation of a new diagnosis, you may tend to slip into the "victim mentality." To regain a fuller perspective, consider your experience thus far from the template of:

- Challenge
- Choice
- Outcome

First, define your *challenges*. What symptoms are you experiencing? What medications have worked or not worked? How has this affected your daily habits and routines? How is this situation imposing limitations, at least temporarily?

If you have experienced depression, frustration, or anger, articulate how these emotions have impacted your life. Perhaps you would include sleeplessness, gastro-intestinal issues, and early fatigue, both physical and mental.

Next, think back to the *choices* you made or are making. You may have chosen to engage in a specific therapy. Perhaps you talked with a counselor, or instituted some new habits and rhythms into your life to combat the challenges you experienced. What choices did you make in response to the challenges that came your way?

Finally, consider the *outcomes*. Have any of these choices resulted in improvement in any way? Even slight improvement counts. The goal is progress, not perfection.

By defining your experience through this template, you may realize several benefits. First of all, these questions force you into an expectant posture of action. You will not sit idly by, while the disease runs its course. Instead, by responding to your challenges with choices, you expect better outcomes.

Furthermore, clarity may emerge. Sometimes the right question helps us cut through the fog to place our finger on the pulse of the problem or the solution.

Besides benefitting you, as you learn to assess and tell your story through the lens of this template, other people may benefit from your model.

Right Now

Before cruising on to chapter seven, jot down some notes about your own story. Or, take some serious time, and write your paragraph. You may find that it is more difficult to write one paragraph than it is to regale your audience with pages of experience.

Write it down. Right now. I'll wait.

Lesson Seven

Find your partners for the journey

Alone we can do so little; together we can do so much.

-Helen Keller

As you well know, your time with a doctor is typically limited. Sometimes severely limited! Therefore, the more prepared you are prior to the visit, the better.

Before your visit, think through the routine of questions that your doctor is likely to ask you and prepare your answers. Also, be sure to write down three questions that you have as well.

Let her know about changes in symptoms or concerns about sleep patterns, anxiety, or any other developments. Ask about new therapies. Repeat back what the doctor has recommended to ensure clarity.

Use this rule of three; three developments since the last time you saw your doctor and three questions. Write them down.

Some patients find it helpful to maintain a journal or binder to keep up with medications, symptoms, questions, and other developments. Whether this takes a written or digital form, you might consider some type of system to stay organized and prepared.

To optimize your communication with your doctor, you might consider some of these questions:

- What does my doctor need to hear from me?

- How can I give the most accurate picture of my symptoms?

- Which daily activities are most important? Enlist your doctor to help you do what you want to be able to keep doing.

Of course, before you see your doctor, you must endure the waiting room. It's not always so bad, just sometimes. I hope you enjoy these observations.

3 People You Meet in the Waiting Room

The lovely and the loathsome are all there.

Waiting rooms. After a cool entrance and sneaky survey of the crowd, you proceed to the desk. Somewhere between completing paperwork and hearing your name called, you learn something about the people around you. While you may have encountered many types, these three are likely encounters:

The kind soul. Ahhh. Even if you or your loved one don't feel like talking, the kind soul allows you to relax. Sensitive not to ask too much or talk too much, this person radiates good energy. Their smile puts you at ease. Their compassion steers clear of pity. And their encouraging words nudge you into a surprisingly appreciative mode. Prescription? Enjoy. Be thankful.

The over sharer. It usually begins with a question, but quickly turns into a hostage situation! You find yourself nodding on the outside, but crying on the inside as your mind races through options to make it stop. It's the old bait and switch. "How are you?" becomes "how I am" …in unnecessary and unsolicited detail. Enduring tales of bunions, horrible reactions, and distant cousins, you pray for your name to be called. But, at least they're somewhat friendly. Prescription? Be kind. Send them well wishes. And pray for your name to be called!

The miserable mope. You will identify them easily by their tone…whiney and loud. It is as if their conversation (even if among their own party) is intended for the entire waiting room. As they talk, they will inevitably complain and make observations on all things inappropriate and in ignorant detail. Prescription? Move! Or, make notes on what you're hearing just for the fun of it.

While you may encounter these three, you are probably more likely to encounter people who are quiet and don't want to be there any more than you do.

But which person are you in the waiting room? Even though less than ideal circumstances have landed you in the waiting room, consider how you can radiate good energy.

Finding the help I didn't want to need

We all need help sometimes.

I would much rather be the helper than the helpee. Like, to a fault. Perhaps you can identify with this.

But, over the past twelve years of my wife's struggle with Dermatomyositis, I have found the help I didn't want to need in the form of:

- A kind and newly widowed lady who insisted on bringing us food in the early weeks of my wife's illness

- An oil and gas company owner and his gracious wife who came to our home to keep our baby and toddler in the middle of the night so

- my wife could take me to the emergency room with a kidney stone

- My parents driving an hour and a half twice a week to help with our young children

- My in-laws opening their home to us when my wife experienced a second health crash

- Meals and kind words from numerous friends several times per year when my wife receives IVIG infusion therapy

- Encouraging words and good breakfast with a man who understands and is 25 years older than I am

- And about 50 other such examples

I am ferociously independent. So, my first reaction is to resist advice, help, or direction. But, every time I find the help I didn't want to need, I am grateful.

Worth Repeating

Until we can receive with an open heart, we're never really giving with an open heart.

-Brene Brown

Back to the Idea of Partners

"Other people matter." I love this simple, yet profound quote from noted Psychologist, Christopher Peterson. These words are at the heart of this chapter.

Peterson says, "It is in the company of others that we often experience pleasure and certainly how we best savor its aftermath." Furthermore, "Good relationships with other people may be a necessary condition for our own happiness, even in markedly individualistic cultures like the contemporary United States."

If you tend towards rugged individualism, this may be a hard pill to swallow.

But think about it. How many good times were such because of the people around you? How many difficult times have been eased by some of those same people?

Our team consists of our families, Dr. Grau, Dr. Targoff, Dr. Crawford, the Myositis Foundation, and others. At times, the team has included physical therapists, online yoga instructors, church groups, and more.

Most likely, you need at least five people or organizations on your team. Think of doctors, specialists, family members, friends, support groups, disease organizations, therapists, counselors, and more.

Who are your partners? **Go ahead and list them here:**

Lesson Eight

Keep learning

Live as if you were to die tomorrow. Learn as if you were to live forever.

-Mahatma Ghandi

Upon diagnosis, some people dive into research and some people avoid any further thought of it for a while. Both responses are quite natural (see chapter one on denial).

In the pursuit of knowledge about a new condition, several things are bound to happen.

First, you will find solid research. However, unless you are trained or accustomed to processing academic journal articles, you may find this body of information to be somewhat inaccessible. Typically, academic research utilizes a very narrow focus and uses technical language.

Second, you will find first hand experiences in the form of books, chat rooms, blogs, etc. Some of these are fabulous. Some just sound crazy!

Third, if you are fortunate, you will also locate a source to interpret the research and join it to practical experience. Often, this type of guidance comes in the form of a kind and intelligent soul at an educational event of the disease organization or perhaps at a support group. Some books excel at practical guidance with encouragement as well.

The next three sections highlight some tools we have learned to put in our toolbox over the past decade.

Enough

She was up again at 2:00 a.m. After a string of nights spent lying awake, plagued by worries and concerns, she finally got up when she awoke.

Knowing that she was likely to repeat her recent pattern and only reap a lack of rest and resolution, she silently crept into a quiet nook of their home.

First, she wrote in her journal, detailing her concerns. Stress at work, financial squeezes, and some relational tensions topped the list. A sense of relief began to emerge as she finally put her finger on the source of her angst.

Then, she analyzed what she could do about any of these items and what it would take to come to peace with them. Much to her chagrin most could not be resolved on this night. Resolution would require asking for advice, recommitting to her daily rhythms of productivity, and engaging a step by step persistence. Getting out of and through these situations would be a process, rather than a magical session of three wishes with the genie in the bottle.

Finally, she practiced a spiritual exercise that she had heard of but never tried. She prayed, "Thank you for giving me enough; enough for today. Thank you for giving me enough love, joy, peace, discipline, courage, energy, and hope. I receive enough for today. Thank you. Amen."

Based on the Bible story of the Israelites being fed manna (bread) in the wilderness each morning, the "enough" prayer demands a focus on one day at a time. As the story is told, the Israelites could only gather enough manna for one day. They couldn't hoard a week's worth. But each morning, there was enough for that day.

As she considered this, she repeated her short, simple prayer over and over until she began to believe it.

She still didn't know how all of these worrisome situations would resolve over time, but as she slipped back into bed, she knew that she had enough to live well for this day.

With a calm mind and restful breathing, she quickly drifted back to sleep.

Mindset Matters

Stanford University Psychologist Carol S. Dweck identifies mindset as a fundamental difference maker in our lives.

On the one hand, a fixed mindset assumes that everything is pre-determined, limited, and unchangeable. This base assumption produces negative self-talk. For instance, *I could never do that, I don't have what it takes, I would never be good at that, I'm not creative enough.* And in most cases, you live right into your limiting beliefs.

On the other hand, Dweck describes the growth mindset. People with a growth mindset tend to believe that they can always learn something new, improve their creativity, and move past mistakes. Their inner dialogue sounds more like, *I can do this, I am learning from this, I will try again.*

Resilience and lifelong learning typify those with a growth mindset. Granted, no one is 100% one or the other, but we do have dominant tendencies that make a substantial difference. Those with a growth mindset push back and re-script their negative messaging into the self-talk of hope, possibility, and courage.

Mindset matters. Especially in care scenarios.

Resistance

For two years, one of Kathy's doctors suggested that she consider a new, innovative treatment for her disease. Since we were experiencing a decent amount of stability and had suffered through a bad response to a particular medicine in the first month of her diagnosis, we resisted.

No thanks.

Then, we attended her national conference and met scores of people who swore to the "liquid gold" of IVIG infusion therapy for Dermatomyositis. We attended a session on this therapy, and chatted with patients and professionals.

While we considered ourselves to be quite informed about living with this condition, we learned so much by placing ourselves in a context of learning. Because of this, Kathy began IVIG infusion therapy and it has been one of the most helpful things she has done thus far.

We are glad we kept learning.

Tools for the Toolbox

Whether you have a woodworking shop, a quilting room, or any type of craft area, can you really ever have too many tools? If you become aware of a new and helpful tool, aren't you likely to find a use for it?

So it is with information and tools to help you de-stress, relax, or nurture your health. When you learn about models to help manage the life of chronic illness and caregiving, you have found a useful tool. Medications, therapies, and innovative methods for treatment all give us hope.

Our learning about the enough prayer, the growth mindset, and hundreds of other such tools has added value to our lives and empowered us to keep going. I suspect the same is true for you.

Keep learning. Continue to add tools to your toolbox.

Lesson Nine

Give and live beyond yourself

We rise by lifting others.

-Robert Ingersoll

Extended illness can leave you focused on your own survival and eventually blinded to the world outside your painful concerns. This is understandable. In fact, this tendency is quite natural.

However, this dynamic leaves you focused inward. Exhausted from energy spent on getting by, a shift to focus energy and time on others can renew your spirits.

As this challenge soaks in, consider the next few observations on living and giving beyond yourself.

700 Years

For 700 years, they've been holding hands.

According to *USA Today*, September 19 2014, "Archaeologists in England digging at a 14th century burial site made an unexpected discovery: A couple buried together holding hands had remained that way all this time." Further evidence from surrounding skeletons suggests a violent or at least dismal situation leading to their deaths and burial.

700 years.

Why?

The scene points to desperation. You're probably already ahead of me in assuming that one of these people grasped the hand of the other prior to their last breath.

Fear. Love. Comfort. This shocking, yet compelling find is loaded with the kind of sentiment that causes us to stop and reflect.

Desperately, lovingly, holding hands in the grimmest of circumstances.

It kind of makes you want to grab the hand of someone you love…and mean it.

Often, giving and living beyond yourself begins with the people closest to you.

Worth Repeating

Immature love says I love you because I need you. Mature love says I need you because I love you.

–Erik Fromm

Fix You

Sometimes, we just can't fix it. We want to, but the dynamics of the situation are beyond our ability to control. The lyrics of this classic song, *Fix You*, by Coldplay, capture this sentiment precisely.

When you try your best but you don't succeed

When you get what you want but not what you need

When you feel so tired but you can't sleep

Stuck in reverse

And the tears come streaming down your face

When you lose something you can't replace

When you love someone but it goes to waste

Could it be worse?

Lights will guide you home

And ignite your bones

And I will try to fix you

If you have a friend in crisis or in a slow downward spiral, do what you can to help. Be a friend. Even if you can't fix it completely, do what you know you can do.

Encourage. Be there. Bring food. Send blessings. Pray. Listen.

Bring the face of one friend to mind. Think about the situation. You'll know what to do.

The Gift of the Half-Eaten Donut

On the last day of Teacher Appreciation Week, students brought their gifts to my wife. In the style of First Graders, they shared what their parents had purchased in combination with their own creations and expressions of love.

One student watched with disappointment. He hadn't brought a present. But even though his mind worked more slowly than most of the other students, the wheels began to turn. Back to this scenario in a moment.

At the beginning of the year, other teachers warned my wife that he would be difficult, that perhaps he would not be able to function in a normal classroom. Facing significant learning and social challenges, he may always struggle.

But my wife loves him as she loves all of her students. I know she loves them, because she tells them that she loves them and she treats them like she loves them. Around our dinner table, we hear her speak of her students with a decisive overtone of love; especially for this student.

Because of her fondness for this student, my son looks out for him and my daughter checked on him in the bus line each afternoon in her role with Safety Patrol. On a recent trip to have lunch with one of my children, I stopped by my wife's classroom and this student came up to share with me what he had learned.

I beamed like a proud father. Even though I've only seen him a few times, I feel like I know him and love him because of the way my wife speaks of him at home.

Now back to the story. As his wheels continued to turn, he noticed a potential gift on his desk. So, he wrapped it carefully, drew a picture with a message that only a loving teacher could decipher, and delivered his gift, proud to be giving like the other children.

And though my wife received many nice things that day, perhaps no gift was greater than the gift of the half-eaten donut.

Worth Repeating

Love is a gift. You can't buy it, you can't find it, someone has to give it to you. Learn to be receptive of that gift.

-Kurt Langner

Mrs. W.

She is more grateful for less than any person

I have ever known, Lord.

All but abandoned by her son,

Forgotten by the church,

Living in a rundown house,

And finally sharing a room in a nursing home.

Sick. Chronically unable to catch her breath, even on the ventilator.

Swollen at the ankles and feet.

Only able to see or hear well at a short distance.

But hopeful and encouraging,

And thankful.

Thankful?

For too few visits,

Poor health

And a hopeless situation.

Yes, she hopes and express gratitude.

I came to encourage her, and she blesses me.

She conveys forgiveness, grace, and wonder.

Lord, surely there is a dark side I don't see.

Curses I don't hear.

I wouldn't blame her.

But all I hear is faith in the valley.

And I am grateful for her.

Amen.

Lost and Found

Gently, the sun warmed my face. The tall pines reflected perfectly in the still water. The wind sang through acres of trees.

No brooding, just good breathing. Perched on top of an old stone spring house by the side of Lost Lake, I sat and allowed my soul to catch a breath.

Then, I heard a twig snap behind me. I turned to find an attractive lady in her mid-40's with a frazzled man in his mid-50's and their very expensive camera and stand. His eyes were wild. I had seen them about four hours earlier as we both climbed around the rocks at Robbers Cave State Park in Wilburton, Oklahoma.

"Where's the $%&*@! cave, man? I mean, do you know how to get from here to the cave?" he asked with increasing volume and then related their futile attempts over the past four hours to find the entrance to Robbers Cave.

I did my best to point them back in the right direction and even help them locate themselves on the map. True, the entrance to the cave is a bit hard to spot and even tougher to reach, but it's only about ten minutes from the parking lot! They had been lost for four hours in their attempts to find it!

He begrudgingly thanked me and hurried off with his wife and camera to continue their tiring quest for the cave. I resumed a great moment in time.

Sometimes you're lost and sometimes you're found.

I hope your path leads you to your desired destination.

Worth Repeating

In the woods is perpetual youth.

–Ralph Waldo Emerson

Finding the Energy You Didn't Know You Had

So this is the paradox. My wife could probably qualify for disability benefits if she wanted. But, she doesn't want to just yet, as of this writing.

And even though teaching first graders sounds like a ridiculously tiring job for someone with an autoimmune disease, and even though that assumption is correct, her teaching actually energizes her in more ways than it de-energizes her.

Teaching children gives her purpose and mission and a way to be of service in the world. She's really good at it and genuinely loves it. I know it's fashionable these days to talk bad about teachers. But, none of the arguments applies to my wife. She works four to five nights a week during the school year. She cries over children, and devises a plan for each child to succeed by the end of the year. She was the Teacher of the Year at her school one year.

And she is living with Dermatomyositis. Living at about 70-80% of where she was before her condition came along. Teaching gives her energy. Sometimes giving and living beyond yourself helps you find the energy you didn't know you had.

Lesson Ten

Create beautiful moments anyway

I don't think of all the misery, but of the beauty that still remains.

-Anne Frank

I fully concur with this elegantly pointed observation from Elizabeth Kubler Ross:

"The most beautiful people we have known are those who have known defeat, known suffering, known struggle, known loss, and have found their way out of the depths. These persons have an appreciation, a sensitivity, and an understanding of life that fills them with compassion, gentleness, and a deep loving concern. Beautiful people do not just happen."

Unlikely Goal

One of the most excruciating limitations for Kathy was not being able to pick up our son, Seth, as a baby. We picked him up and put him in her arms, and as he grew more mobile, she helped him scramble up into her arms. Simply picking up your toddler was something Kathy had lost the physical strength to manage.

When she started physical therapy, her Therapist asked, "What do you want to be able to do? Not how much do you want to lift, but what do you want to do?"

"I want to be able to pick up my son," she replied.

This is no one's goal. No one places this item on a to do list, bucket list, or any other type of dream list.

Unless you can't do it.

After six months of physical therapy, when our son was closing in on three years old and growing too big for almost anyone to pick him up, she did it!

With wrapping paper and presents strewn around the living room at a Christmas gathering of family, Seth got excited about one of his gifts from us. He ran over to Kathy with expectant celebration as any young child would do, but backed off as he had learned to be careful around mom.

"No, come here buddy!" Kathy encouraged. And she bent down and put her arms under his arms as he wrapped his around her neck. She straightened up holding her son!

And the room fell quiet for a brief, sacred moment as we all witnessed what we had never seen in his young life. Tears welled up in her mother's eyes and mine too. Excited conversation started up again as we expressed gratitude for what had just happened.

She reached her goal just in time. She picked up our son. And it was a profoundly beautiful moment.

Create Beautiful Moments Anyway

Not every day is full of "bluebirds on your shoulder."

Problem finders, negative people, and fussy folks bump into us. Stuff happens. Not all of it ideal.

Create beautiful moments anyway.

Take a moment, take a hike, or take someone you love on an ice cream date.

One of the most life-giving habits for our family has been the date/adventure. Twice a month, I take my daughter and my wife on dates, and I take my son on adventures. We do this at least twice a month. This rhythm has been crucial for us.

From smoothies to movies to hikes and bike rides, these outings allow for one on one time. Yes, we must ruthlessly carve these into the schedule.

Sometimes I should be doing a chore or accomplishing some other task. But, this is more important.

After more than a decade of my wife living with a chronic condition, we are still determined to create beautiful moments ANYWAY!

I hope you find ways to generate beauty, even in the midst of less than ideal circumstances.

Worth Repeating

Creativity takes courage.

-Henry Matisse

When Seasons Change

Pause to reflect when seasons change.

Sometimes it happens in September, sometimes in October. But, it always catches my attention and invites me into a reflective mood.

The first cool day of fall, when it starts out cool and rainy and stays that way all day. Typically, this is not a productive day of work for me. I embrace the quiet, find a reason to walk outside, and turn off email for extended periods of time.

This day nudges my thoughts into a review of the year thus far, how I'm tracking on my yearly goals, and heightens my senses about what or who I may be missing.

This physical day of weather change and its spiritual and emotional effect remind me to reflect and appreciate other types of season changes.

For instance, you might pause to reflect on a significant season of life spent in a certain town, job, or relationship. Perhaps, you would reflect on years of debt now paid off, or a specific house, or a season of life with a group of friends who has since moved on.

As cool, rainy days approach your part of the country, hit the pause button on your hectic life. Reflect. Mourn. Celebrate.

When seasons change.

Appreciative for Love

Recently, I heard this interesting perspective on our postures toward love:

The young are excited and enamored with the possibilities of love.

The middle-aged tend to often be disillusioned.

And the old are appreciative for love.

While these descriptions may be severely overgeneralized, I think this makes sense. And, I am deciding now (at the ripe old middle age of 43) to go ahead and transition to the third stage.

I want to be appreciative for love.

And I think I am. I appreciate my wife's friendship. Through joy and through struggle, we've been able to talk about everything. I appreciate her warmth, concern, humor, and mischievousness!

Even at this early point in life, I suspect that I could think back and savor thousands of moments.

How about you?

Worth Repeating

Love is a choice.

–Leo Buscaglia

The Dissonant Harmony of Happy and Sad

Making peace with paradox. It's tough, but essential for better living and better perspective.

She received infusion treatments on her birthday. This was decidedly NOT the way she wanted to spend her birthday. But, her parents brought cake anyway. And the nurse joined in the celebration. Sadness and happiness had collided.

This same experience happens in groups as well. While one person enjoys remission and fewer meds, another person just received the bad news. As one caregiver finally gets to take a vacation, another struggles to pull herself out of the monotony of a deteriorating situation.

So, what do you do?

- Be sensitive to the people around you, but enjoy your good times.
- Broaden your view. Remember that joy and pain are often parallel, connected…two parts of a greater whole.

When times are tough, it is difficult to focus on gratitude. Try anyway.

Making peace with paradox. Easier said than done. But, as you make the attempt, you may just hear the dissonant harmony of happy and sad.

Worth Repeating

The curious paradox is that when I accept myself just as I am, then I can change.

-Carl Rogers

As you work to create and receive beautiful moments, you meet people who remind you to do so.

Happy People

Her energy and enthusiasm precede her greeting. She is the founder and owner of Vintage Coffee and she knows my order. Small decaf Americano, perhaps with a chocolate covered biscotti.

I tend to gravitate toward exceptional baristas. Whether they are caffeinated or not, I do not know. But, I appreciate their infectious energy. And at this coffee shop in my new routine, her energy is noticeable.

He makes a difference every time he comes to our office. He is living with Parkinson's and must be careful to time his medication just right to make it through voice therapy or choir rehearsal.

But for whatever may be going wrong in his world, he enters our doors to make things better for other people. And, I am grateful for the seeds of joy that he sows.

He has a new story every time we talk! His great success in politics, business, and higher education has been interspersed with seasons of significant struggle.

Yet, he still has new stories! He may have been down, but he didn't stay down.

And perhaps that is one of my primary observations about happy people: they get back up and live again anyway.

Worth Repeating

The best way to pay for a lovely moment is to enjoy it.

-Richard Bach

Beyond Compare

Beauty is here, now, anyway.

Three years ago, he ran a marathon.

Today, he received treatments for bone cancer.

At age 36, this is not what he had planned. Not even on the map. With two toddlers, a young wife, and scary circumstances, he has done a lot of comparing.

His mind races with comparisons of what he thought life would be like, what it used to be like, and what some fellow cancer patients' lives are like. Inevitably, he compares his life with the seemingly carefree lives of his thirty-something friends.

Each one of these comparisons is completely natural and to be expected. Who wouldn't have these thoughts?

But, he decides that at present, these veins of thought are causing him more misery than comfort. So, he switches gears.

He eases back into the present; the precious present.

A contented smile betrays the joy found immediately in the moment as he listens to one toddler sing and watches the other one operating his tablet. "They are so smart at such a young age," he thinks.

Then, his thoughts move to the kitchen, where he catches a glimpse of his wife washing dishes since their dishwasher is broken. "She hasn't even complained about that," he surmises. "I guess she knows we have more important things going on. She is beautiful inside and out."

And that lump forms in his throat.

But it's okay. Even though so much is not okay in his world, at this precise moment, he is good. All comparisons aside, he rests into the present.

Love completely engulfs him. And it is good.

Lesson Eleven

Determination is required.

Keep going when you don't feel like it.

Success is the sum of small efforts, repeated day in and day out.

-Robert Collier

I wish I could tell you that dealing with months, years or decades of life with chronic illness and caregiving will be easy. But it won't.

As has been posited so many times already in this book, it's not *either/or*, but rather *both/and*.

In the spirit of truth telling, let's take a moment to focus on the necessary place of determination.

She keeps going

Her voice is soft. Her attempts at annunciation tend to leave her words slurred together due to the effects of Parkinson's disease.

She walks slowly, precariously on the verge of a fall at any moment. The disease has progressed significantly over the years, robbing her of many functions that the rest of us take for granted.

Most would have given up by now; but not her.

With what mobility and life she has in her, she just keeps showing up...to exercise group, LOUD crowd voice therapy group, and various events.

Sometimes she arrives with scratches and bruises betraying a recent fall, but she dismisses the pain and keeps going. Even though she appears to need help, she insists on helping and caring for others in the group at every meeting. Adversity is no match for her indomitable spirit. And even when she eventually succumbs one of these days to the physical degenerative effects of Parkinson's, the disease still will not have defined her.

Faith, courage, and determination define her.

And I am thankful to witness such determination week after week.

Worth Repeating

The difference between the impossible and possible lies in a man's determination.

-Tommy Lasorda

Challenges

It takes determination to live with a chronic illness. And determination is required to persevere in caregiving.

I realize this is not a major news flash for you, but it does serve as a reminder. When you wake up hurting every day with limitations on your physical ability or questions about your longevity, a sense of grit keeps us going. When you drive through the pharmacy one more time, or take off work for a doctor's appointment one more time, your resolve keeps you going.

The experience of chronic illness wears on you.

Another new sore...

One more bad test result...

A new symptom...

Getting your hopes up for an innovative treatment that fails to deliver...

Medical bills...

More blood work...

Ahhh! That bloody blood work...

Errors on medical bills...

Insensitive workers in the health care world...

And just feeling sick.

These and many more take their toll. They wear us down; mentally, emotionally, spiritually, and physically.

And this is the reason that an inner sense of determination is so crucial. Our inner fortitude reminds us to push through, to reframe, and to keep going.

Pushing Through

I have witnessed my wife pushing through for twelve years now.

Stuck on a low chair, quivering legs, struggling to get out of the bathtub, determined to open a bottle cap and even keeping an opener in her purse to help.

I have watched her work and not complain, teach and not make excuses about her illness. I have witnessed her toiling into the night during the school year, working weekends.

When my children asked why she was working one Saturday morning, I told them that she is the best because she works harder than some of those other teachers who gripe and complain. You don't see their cars up here do you? Appropriately, my wife was selected as teacher of the year at her school the following year, ten years into her illness.

This, when she could probably be on disability. One day, she probably will be, and I don't begrudge anyone else for utilizing the disability system...at least when they are legitimately disabled. But, I am proud of my wife for doing what she can do as long as she can do it.

Most mornings she doesn't feel like getting up at 5:45 a.m. to go to work. But she pushes through. The daily tasks that most of us take for granted are difficult or impossible for her, but she pushes through with creative solutions.

I know she receives unfair condescension from some lesser human beings because of her visible skin redness and calcifications, but she pushes through and refuses to be angry. As you can tell, I am angry for her. She lives on occasion with open sores that refuse to heal, but she pushes through. Her hair has thinned, but she pushes through.

My wife pushes through with determination. And I am thoroughly proud of her. She is much tougher than I am.

As I have met hundreds of families dealing with all sorts of health adversity, I have seen patients pushing through.

And they have my complete admiration.

See a better future

What does determination look like on the ground? It looks like the 54-year-old early onset Parkinson's patient, trained as a geologist, who now gives piano lessons for other Parkinson's patients.

It looks like one of the piano students, an 88-year-old former architect who is living with Parkinson's, but taking piano lessons!

Or, the brain cancer survivor who now counsels people battling brain cancer.

Or, the caregiver whose loved one passed away four years ago, but re-emerged as a light for her friend's journey, taking her to support groups and conferences about her disease.

Or, a former elementary principal who lives with Parkinson's, but organizes other Parkinson's patients who are struggling with their voice volume to go read books to developmentally disabled children.

Or, the young mother living with an autoimmune disease who fights through the pain to continue working and providing for her family.

Or, the lady who has cared for two parents with Alzheimer's and now prepares to care for her husband, whose memory issues are becoming undeniable.

Seeing a better future does not happen easily. Sometimes it even requires reframing.

Reframing

For a moment, I paused. With intention, I filled my nostrils and lungs with the cool, moist air of a Tennessee spring day.

My eyes landed on dogwoods just beginning to bloom, red bud trees already splashing the landscape, and the pronounced hint of green on the trees as far as I could see. Listening to song-birds playing their tunes, I smiled contentedly, thinking that I might just be enjoying the perfect spring day, playing golf with my dad at the Tennessee River Golf Course.

Then I heard two more distinct sounds.

The crack of a 7-iron hitting the ball…and the splash of a golf ball hitting the water.

The smile went away, but quickly turned into laughter.

Before we got back in the golf cart, I added another ball to the collection at the bottom of the pond.

Nevertheless, no lack of golfing skill could ruin a day of excellent scenery and enjoyable company.

And that's called re-framing. Some might allow mediocre golf skills to ruin a great day, but I don't do that anymore. In fact, I find that life demands quite a lot of re-framing. And that's okay. It's a skill worth learning, especially in the spring.

Worth Repeating

If a problem can't be solved within the frame it was conceived, the solution lies in reframing the problem.

-Brian McGreevy

A Few More Things About Re-framing

When used properly, this technique does not deny difficult reality. However, re-framing is useful in helping us regain a fuller view of reality. Re-framing helps when we focus exclusively on the negative, which is usually only part of reality. Observe your own thought patterns. Ask yourself, "How can I re-frame my view and understanding of this situation?"

One

You can do one thing right now.

Sure, you have lots of things to do. You have a gajillion emails, meetings, and projects to finish if you could ever quit going to meetings. You have things at home to clean, fix, and maintenance. You have people to call, goals to reach, and fires to put out. You may be living on empty.

But right now, you can do one thing.

Make a list with two columns. In one column write down the things you're worried about and need to do. Then, in the other column, write down the one thing you are choosing to do right now. Just one.

If that one thing takes close to an hour, take a 5-10 minute break. Then do the next one thing.

If your life is out of control, stressful, and overwhelming, try this little exercise in managing multiple tasks. Forget multi-tasking. Current research is disproving its effectiveness.

One.

One task at a time. One thing at a time. One hour at a time.

One.

Worth Repeating

It is vain to do with more what can be done with less.

-William of Occam (1300-1350) originator of "Occam's Razor"

And all of this brings us back to a reminder about the determination and resilience that reside deep within you.

5 Keys to Tapping Your Inner Grit

You have the capacity for resilience!

When difficult circumstances flood around you, clarity and success may seem elusive. To take back control, consider these five keys to tapping your inner grit:

Put your finger on the problem. At 3:00 a.m. with worries swirling amidst your attempts to get back to sleep, all issues seem slippery. I recommend that you get up and write down a list of what is bugging you. Identifying and naming your problem causes the swirling to cease and moves you in the right direction.

Chunk it down. Often, the problem is not just one, but many. Easily, we can become overwhelmed. So, chunk it down into what needs to be done in phase one, two and three, or focus only on what you can tackle today.

Take action. Identify the first thing and do it. Feelings of depression and anxiety are at least altered when you take action. What can you do right now to move towards a solution?

Make the ask. One of these early actions may involve asking someone else to weigh in, consult, or do something you can't do. Who do you need to ask?

Remind yourself that you CAN do the next right thing. You have enough energy, peace, love, etc. to do the next right thing. You have the capacity for resilience and you have the grit to do one thing. You can't do 172 tasks related to a move right now. But, you can take action on the first one!

These certainly aren't the only five measures to tapping your inner grit, but these five will get you moving. Whatever you are facing or whatever challenge is plaguing you, I encourage you to tap your inner grit as you live through it!

You can live with determination. Yes, it is tough. But, you can do it, one step at a time.

Lesson Twelve

There is grace for you

Ideas come to people who are receptive to them.

-Lawrence Block

Have you forgiven yourself lately? Really, just given yourself some slack?

Before you bristle or dismiss this chapter as meddlesome, I have a confession. I have not been a flawless caregiver. In fact, at some points I have been a rather reluctant, disengaged caregiver. Sure, I know better, but I have not always done better.

So, I have had to ask forgiveness from my wife at times and start fresh. I have had to acknowledge the truth of my own disappointments, and give myself some grace. But first, a few thoughts on forgiving others.

On forgiving others

"When we forgive, we take back control of our own fate and our feelings. We become our own liberators. We don't forgive to help the other person. We don't forgive for others. We forgive for ourselves," Desmond Tutu bluntly describes.

For caregiver and patient, hurts will occur. Notice I did not say that they might occur. They will. If you haven't been hurt or offended by a close family member or spouse, you either haven't been paying attention or you haven't been doing this for very long!

"There is no way of living with other people without, at some point, being hurt," Desmond Tutu states.

Of course, it would be difficult to say much more about forgiveness without some clarity on the subject. Again, Bishop Tutu helps us.

"Forgiveness does not erase accountability. It is not about turning a blind eye or even turning the other cheek. It is not about letting someone off the hook or saying it is okay to do something monstrous. Forgiving is simply about understanding that every one of us is both inherently good and inherently flawed. Within every hopeless situation and every seemingly hopeless person lies the possibility of transformation."

I can live with that definition. How about you?

Forgiving Ourselves

Often, the person who most needs our forgiveness is us. It seems to me that this may be the least exercised spiritual practice. Forgiving self. Even more rare than forgiving others, which I suspect is woefully lacking for most.

This one may be trickier. While I may be quick to forgive others for minor slights, or even eventually forgive more significant grievances, I don't often think to forgive myself. It just doesn't occur to me.

So, I live with it. For long periods of time.

Some of us are accustomed to such a shame based way of life and way of viewing ourselves, that a wholesale personality overhaul would require years or decades. But nevertheless, the spiritual, mental, and emotional exercise of forgiving ourselves generates much-needed peace and renewal.

The reasons for forgiving ourselves are the same as for forgiving others. It is how we become free of the past. It is how we heal and grow. It is how we make meaning out of our suffering, restore our self-esteem, and tell a new story of who we are. Once again, Bishop Tutu hits the point squarely on the head.

Defining the Issue

For what would you possibly forgive yourself?

- Resenting your patient. Specifically, resenting the medical bills or their lack of effort in exercise, therapy, or nutrition.
- You might resent that you have to do more of the work around the house.
- Or, that you have to sacrifice your energy and time in ways that you never imagined were part of the deal.

If any of this type of resentment has built up in your soul, identify it and release it. Forgive it. Start over. Forgive yourself.

Maybe caregiving has led to less energy. Still, you're left with a conundrum because you did change your expectations for yourself. You still expect to exercise like an elite athlete, work 60+ hours per week, and enjoy the adventure in life at the pace of a typical 21-year old. (Maybe these just apply to me?) Has it occurred to you that this may not be realistic? While you're living with a sense of resentment or guilt or shame over not accomplishing all that you want to achieve, might this be unfair? If you are the patient, perhaps the same is true.

That's a good question. About fairness. We are quick to identify unfairness interpersonally, but are you being fair with yourself?

So again, for what would you possibly forgive yourself?

For getting sick in the first place? Did you live an exquisitely healthy life? I doubt it. Did you indulge in too many sweets, colas, and other bad food? Probably. But does this really mean that you must live with excessive guilt? No. The reasons that we get sick are many; from environmental causes to personal choices and genetic predispositions and much more.

Forgiving is difficult, especially forgiving yourself. Have you messed up in some ways? Certainly. Is it just okay? No, of course not. But, you can still forgive yourself and grant yourself a fresh start.

Hopefully, these brief observations have been helpful, but living into it requires extensive practice.

As you lean into it, remember, there is grace for you! If no one else has ever extended it, or if you have a supremely difficult time believing it, allow me to extend some grace to you:

You are forgiven.

Today is a new day, a fresh start.

There is more than enough grace to go around, and right now, I am telling you that there is grace for you.

Receive it.

This notion is greater than any one religion. This is a universal principle and reality.

There is grace for you.

Even in your most wretched moments, you are full of beauty and wonder.

There is grace for you. It is yours. Receive it.

Conclusion

Both/And, rather than either/or.

You are living with two parallel realities, two parallel truths. Part of your experience in caregiving and living with a difficult condition is frustrating, maddening, depressing, and difficult.

But this is not the only reality. At the same time, you may also experience beauty, love, peace, kindness, and courage.

Just as I stood on the Galveston beach witnessing a great paradox: impending storm from one direction, breathtaking sunrise from the other, and dolphins frolicking off the shore. I recommend that you embrace the paradox of life in a care situation as best you can.

Easily, you will notice the more challenging aspects of your life. But, lean in to find the beauty as well. As you do, I hope you will join me in the valiant attempt to live with resilience.

And thrive anyway.

Endnotes

Chapter One

7 *Denial helps us to pace our feelings of grief* Elisabeth Kubler Ross and David Kessler, *On Grief and Grieving: Finding the Meaning of Grief Through the Five Stages of Loss,* (Scribner, 2005), 10.

8 *the ability to rebound from crisis* Froma Walsh, *Strengthening Family Resilience* (The Guilford Press, 2006), ix.

8-9 *ordinariness of resilience* "Ordinary Magic. Resilience processes in development", *The American Psychologist* (March 2001): 227-238.

11-12 *Someone once asked Ray Charles* Ted Leeson, *The Habit of Rivers* (Lyons Press, 2006), 109ff.

Chapter Two

24-25 *Expressions of positive emotions have numerous interpersonal benefits* "Willingness to Express Emotions to Caregiving Spouses", *NIH Public Access (December 2009): 1-9*.

26 *a process of changing identity* "Caregiving as a Process of Changing Identity: Implications for Caregiver Support", *Journal of the American Society on Aging* (Spring 2009): 47-52.

28-29 *53% of caregivers report* Mickey Hinds, *Life Senior Services Vintage Magazine* (June 2015), insert.

Chapter Three

43 *A person is a person through other persons* Desmond Tutu, *God is not a Christian*, (Harper One, 2011), 25.

Chapter Four

48 *They talk about the love they felt,* Kerry Egan, The Mayo Clinic Guide to Stress-Free Living, (De Capo Lifelong Books, 2013), Kindle edition.

Chapter Six

66 *Challenge, choices, outcomes*

This helpful model comes from Bill Moyer's program "How to tell your story of self" with credit given to 350.org workshops. To learn more, visit http://workshops.350.org/toolkit/story/.

Chapter Twelve

115-117 *When we forgive, we take back control* Desmond Tutu, *The Book on Forgiving*, (HarperOne, 2014), 16.

.

Schedule Bruce to Speak

Email Bruce directly at:

Bruce@BruceMcIntyre.com

What People Are Saying

"Excellent info and speaker!"

"Wonderful and uplifting! So glad he came here to present."

"He was entertaining while giving very helpful information."

"Very engaging speaker!"

www.BruceMcIntyre.com

Made in the USA
Lexington, KY
22 May 2017